Wander Poems

Dedicated to all those beings

who are poets in their heart of hearts

A man set sail is like a little word
when freed of sentences
he needs no plague of pages
can wing his way towards a morrow
by not even stirring a finger
and become a resounding shout
heard to the ends of the earth and back
he can stay at home and still go to India
can have his cat his art and all of that
and in full silence can speak his heart

Boundless Ocean Mother,
in all the poems written by Your son,
You are just the one wavy line
- incorruptible hum of orchestra
beneath the scram of music (howled),
unremitting bleep of awareness
which yet sent the world into the spin of sleep,
unthinkable like the blue above,
un-killable like the fairy-tale songbird
whose a hundred trillion tunes
name the game fix the price
and never lose the dice...
Oh passionate stone-melting Sun!
You are the eternal mother song-bird,
whose haunting trill is just a stage device.
How could You grieve really

if You are never scattered?
Many necklaces, one neck,
never unstrung or shattered.
A million suits of skin for casual wear,
each one able to be stepped into,
and out of, enjoyed in the mirror
then dismissed, hung to dry,
and ironed separately, naughtily or nice,
a million kinds of making love.
Passionate lover song-bird,
please never leave off your singing!
The trees cannot be quiet because of You
every leaf has its own passport
because of You I cannot sleep
because of listening to all their names.
Because of You lovers lie breathlessly
and want to catch the sky on fire
with the sparks of their skin.
Oh because of You all that is good
is not always true,
all that is bad is not always bad,
I cannot ask for answers
if I should follow You.
The wisest way would be not to pause
to be sane at all but to eat like a pig
and go through with it like a thread
in the needle's eye.
I am a weaver of words.
I pluck them from their mother earth,
bind hearts' wounds with them,
made with one pottage as thick as silence.
I give their food to hungry mouths,
all by one artful thread which holds

my limbs in one piece and gives my voice its reason.
Listen!
This is the clicking of the chill wind,
the lady of the loom downstairs which weaves the
world.
Every morning pass by all the sons of men,
the souls which seek the river, and the newly dead.
But she, the loom-mistress, doesn't turn a hair,
she doesn't lift a finger from the cloth of meditation.
She is the wind that shows the days their facts,
and I am the student of her inspiration.

unborn day
rain upon
this willing hour
your balsamic rain

drum up
your army of laughing droplets
and raining notes
within your silence

echo your song
gush up your fountain
of rainbow sparks
flow down your lava
from the mountain
of your stillness

Train man to conserve
baby in a playpen,
his own rhino reserve
in an Indian mayhem.

Teach man to grow
a secret wild garden,
that wonder to know
expects no return.

Lure the woman in a man
to the bed of free Love.
This is the only plan
I have received from above.

Eyes full of midnight
births of the old ones
they hold a lantern of love
in the keep of your face
feed the lost with their kindness
leave no place for nights of disguise
expose the lies of the bravest.

From Now On
until the next moment,
shoots the silver arrow,
glides the snake glistening,
runs the race of prairie grass,
and though the world is naked,
it hides itself.
Stillness spins its quickening cloak,
and in the flash of the arrow,
the swish of the snake past,
the rustle of the long grass,
the stillness speaks in a rush we cannot grasp,
the wandering way goes on.

LET GO

I let go for this is the day to drink of the sky.
I let go by being sure to hold its infinite cup to my lips
when no public no honours or dollars need to exist.
I let go a stream of all my suppositions
brimful with their brainy bubbles.
I let go my teams of thought-slaves
employed to build towers on shifting sands.
I let go all this will of giving birth,
all my children of invention
liable to crumble or be exploded.
I let go my plans
being only of the nature of old season-tickets.
I let go my hopes,
heaps of dead leaves surely to be kicked.
I let go my stream of being with some celebration,
like ribbons and flags of flesh in festive season,
inner contradictions in the form of helium-filled
intestines,
sneaky twinges of shame nailed to flag-poles
and fluttering gaily in the sky.
I let go my mouth-shat crap
and my life accumulation of tons of obstinate rigor,
into the wind of rage that blows from the heart of the
void,
that they may be consumed.
A roaring volcano of Life, a day of full stillness and
solace,
I let go all the protest marchers...
there are no governments here to bring down,
they have been liberated by the superior rule of
emptiness.

I let go my creaking floorboards, my complaining
endless walls,
my neurotic tinny roof, and my lazy foundations,
to the fangs of the scowling bulldozer.
I let go my old jaundiced eye that has grown its useless
bones in me,
I offer myself uncomplaining as dust in the holy
cremation soup.
I let go on a dark night, where the flood of all
ignorance boils,
I make a libation of poison to join the compost vision
of integration,
and become the mountain-sky of wisdom.
I let go so well that no time is left to taste the remains.
The judgement-trumpet of surrender blows all to the
ends of the earth!
There are no faces left on crouching shoulders.
There are no hidden corners of guilt.
Confusion is replaced by the sound of Ah.
I let go so that the lost land of treasure
is found in the middle of the scrapyard jungle,
and the spineless life of a creeping spirit
is re-clothed with strange grace on a day of eternity
His sins are redeemed. Forgive him! He was me!
I let go so that all within is without, all that is without
is within.
I let go so that all dense longing becomes a feast of
enlightened senses.
I let go so that despair is torn up like the weeds, for it
has no roots.
I let go into the face that smiles even though life is
sadness.

I let go by dying into death, by joining light and
darkness.
I let go both by laughing and by crying.
I let go by not becoming and by not trying.
Drink with me the sky-cup of all this feast
and join my nothingness!

Swiftling cloud, gaily come,
you are the flag of the wind
unfurling here
a jewelled cloth of shower rain.

But your special gift
is "disappearing."
Inspire me with the song that sings
silently inside me as the soundless sky
of the cloud that loves to die!

Swiftling cloud, gaily gone,
your swiftness makes all weakness strong.
It makes me aware of being destroyed,
but without despair,
simply like a summer snow-flake,
first fabricated, then scattered,
dissolved upon the unknown stone.

I stumbled on my climb,
and now I'm coming down the mountain.
I'm coming down like the rain,
down to the valley of my blood.

I stumbled on a stone.
I tripped up well and good.
Yes it was my own lie
so I'm coming down the mountain.

That sliver of a snake
was my own pride
I glimpsed as it slid away
to the dust heap of the past.

I stumbled on the truth of who I am
and wonder knows no shame.
I'm coming down like the rain,
down to the valley of my blood.

Fact of knowing you
like a big speckly stone...
because its fact is sure,
I can afford to feel uncertain.

It causes me to stop and stare
and ask you who and why,
and waver upon the brim
of my automatic smile.

Paradox of knowing you
so stilly standing there
like a jewel or like a boulder
- sometimes causes me to growl.

Paradox of loving you,
union not one nor two...
karma that does not wash away,
bond and gulf of stone.

I am the old heaven's customer upon the hill,
welcomer of last light and life without leaven,
holding no hope, enduring lonely,
instilled with rhythm of skeleton;
seeing that the grace of the year is given,
speaking silence only.

Ever more like my body
is the sailing raft
is the tent-shaped room
with one window and rafters.

Ever more like my spirit is the air
which breathes in and out
by the open attic window
and surges into sky.

Everyday more uncaring
am I swept into stillness
where blue heaven itself
reaches down and steers
this floating triangular room.

The watch
of sleeping pendulums...
and a lone survivor snores,
waiting for the sweeping arc
of a timely sword
to cleave his thought.

Meanwhile the days are full
in scrapped-heart land.
A poem's sprig,
the goad of a honeyed word,

blossoms in the twisted iron.
Some love is learned,
licked off the razor-blade
of a line of pain
and salvaged from the chorus
of circular sentences.
And a woman is there
who's selling fire
for melting down the rusted voices
of my soul into tiny jewels.

Buddha face hangs by single thread,
transforms into ball of crumpled paper
written with words of consolation
kicked from door to door
on the street of hard knocks,
and I follow suit
pummeling the air with tiny fists
reborn from ashes of other messages.
Buddha mouth hangs onto its smile
but only just, sailing up into sky
above the ripped up road full of entrails
of bared pipes and secret domes.
And Life goes on in the same old drains.

Holy Word awaken me!
I am the isolated and frozen ray of sun,
embedded blade within a rock
since kingdom of Ego come.
Upon the power of myself I wait,
upon the words which melt the mental state
of stone.

upon the rain

To be
is to be me.
To be me
is to be alone.
To be alone
is to be free.
To be is just
to Be.
To be alone
is a price.
To be two
is a gift.
Alone,
all alone,
but if given you
I'll rejoice!

I am a happy molehill
and keep the mole in me warm
with thick crumbling loam
and a pile on a shiny lawn
and a seat for peeking out
and a tunnel for arriving far.

I am a happy molehill
made of claw-feet will
at home with my special skill
for turning up on perfect days
when someone's back is turned.

I release all that I think I am
have nothing left to become.
Now the answer I have been waiting for
is Your silence that seals my lips.

GRINDSTONE

I'm paralyzed from being shriveled up
and mean inside.
I'm deaf because I've listened
to the wrong advice and for too long.
I'm dead because of living without "dying."

So turn the grindstone of perplexity
like a wheeling eye of wonder
it may become
like a bird turning in its very wing
like a seed that is swollen with a tree.

So turn the grindstone of perplexity
to sharpen the instrument of concern
to point it to the place of pain;
skillfully release the poison and the pain
from the septic recesses of your childhood.
Understand how like everyone you've been wronged
and still burn in bitter condemnation
of someone you innocently loved who did you harm,
and the whole world burns like you
in the age-old nuclear war of want
- the injury of never being understood,
the poignancy of being all alone
without knowing why.

So turn the grindstone of perplexity
to sharpen the point of your concern;
observe the mass of people suffering,
crying out in being divided;
stir up the bottom of Life's cauldron,

and bring to light the poison in your pleasure;
reflect that if there's so much
in one single person
how much more will there be
in the whole universe put together?
Compassion will surely come.

The solemn face of Buddha
steering
slowly
like
a
ship made of the world

        shaking
       out
         a
        satin
           sail.

I have been nailed
to the unwelcome cross.
I have been sent on a suicide mission
to the bottom of myself.
Unsmiling muses have nursed
the dreams revealed in my doodles,
the hotchpotch of hopes created.

I have been spat like a meteorite
hurtled down from the sky
by the earnest force of my own gravity.

In a place where growling creatures in the sky
show their silver bellies and their sign of crosses
swishing by at certain times of day with whistling thunder,
I am someone seen far away in the distance
just like those aeroplanes above flying to somewhere
yonder.

a drumstick for an Adam
on fire with hidden decision
this soft hot day of life-love

his empty face of swimming pool
squared off by suffered limits
carried on baby shoulders

in warm lush of Java
where I cannot find him
but he sees his ship ahead
sailing between two clashing rocks

One kind of sky
is fragrant within
just why that is
don't ask me.
Since it pervades me
and I once sought to escape it,
now humbly I seek it.
Since it endures in me
and I had no endurance,
now Love requires it.

curly boy
bubble
into sky of chance
gambled away his life
over the dim edge of day
under the lovers' bed

is gone
and I have risen
from my heart-gorged corpse
covered in the seaweed of warm rain
caressed by the ever kiss-filled night
draped in the soft swirl of tidal flesh
and born again

look the velvet sea of earth is mine
spread beneath a sprouting moon
look the tender spring of earth is mine
drawn from the loins of outstripped winter

I am Duration, You are Life.
I am drunken with your extinction.
I am heavy with the hand of fortune.
I was before You and I came to Your burial.
I am the great Idea, the great dream of Time,
borne in the bliss of a mushroom cloud
and ruling by my very terror.
I tire You with my clinging shadow
hanging on the shoulder of Your lover,
I catch You out with a maze of names
and define You into particles of sand....

until You rebel with Your heart of storm
and ring the world awake with living wind
and sound the bell within the deathly shape
and spring with laughter from the bowels of silence
and catch the phantom robber in his invented moment
and bring him to the justice of all Creation.

On the last ground of dogs
in the first land of lepers
where the dog spelled correctly
is a god and the maimed
lift up their new perfect limbs
and birth meets death
in no-man's land
and pool their luck together...
in this place of all-return
and estrangement and rejoicing
please me my guest forever.

On the last ground of Ego
in the first flame of Love,
lime-green vegetation appears
a-sprouting in mad dogs' ears,
the colour of life's insanity
or is it that that's your fear?
Your heart grows wings and flies
because it refuses to be "yours";
it drops a bomb of wonder
and opens worldly eyes.

We who live in the night
knew nothing of the sun's glory
until the fair weather moon arose
and compassionately looked down on us
for our plight was great.

Beholding her in all her forms
soothed the dark dismay of midnight,
grew in us the hope of daylight
and restored our knowledge
of the power of the sun,
blazing in the lost part of the sky.

When we were young,
she fished us with a tender crescent-hook;
when we were older,
she gave us a silver nugget as a promise;
now when we are old,
she loves us with a full shining orb
until we know how to receive,
by the moon-like face of the guru,
what is beyond our power.

Upon the orb of a heart's egg
my love is patiently sitting.
For many long years
the thick shell has slept
in mirror-like calm.
But tomorrow is a day
that comes with a sword.

I am a tree of great difficulty
growing where all is easily still.
My unaccustomed arms are not used
to what they hold.
A slightest breeze makes me madly moan.
Un-free to cling, yet how hard I wish
to keep what I have suffered for
- a golden cloud of leaves.

Lips let loose their tongues,
and words become undone.
What was before is long behind...
this secret night of sweetness
covers this lovers' weakness,
and lets no one think to have a peep
of what's in store ahead...

for we shall be always young.

To bow down my head,
I need some confusion,
like the chicken
needing grit for its egg
and for bigness of Love,
I beg to become small,
tiny in fact as a sandy speck
in the speckle of an egg.

Once in the light of the End
the beginning was a wimp
in a cold sweat
and produced no buds
and heroes walked divided
like mermaids with new legs
and I called out for more control
but felt life was a losing struggle.

Once in the light of the End
the daylight was long in the tooth
and the soul-bird a thing
of too few feathers
to fly the heaviness of heart
and I was like a broken jar of crystal
spilled into diverse lights
on the rack of advancing night.

Once in the light of the End
a simple apple for example
took out a life insurance
and contrived its shine,
and lovers were bitten
as they kissed their lips,
and I was an author (alas!)
whose love was still bitter and slept.

Jonathan Jo
that mouth like an O
that ear like some shell

do you remember they said
dreams could be poured
into your head
to make you too old
and solemn and cold
so to lie as if dead
deep under road
before you could wake
and make a jail break
and become who you were
with the face of surprise
all wonder with its roving eye!

old moon lost nugget rolled out of view
fine blade of thought of before
now rusted in its sheath
night music bass plastered all over
world rounded out ever more hollow

and my cat plays its stick
and my eyes court this screen
like birds that shiver in their nests of pre-dawn.
Oh how are we here and where do we hail from?
and who is our lord if it is not the king of sleep?

minutes of a long night
ousted from a bus station
countdown to eventual release
bowed heads into luggage
car tires swish
gulls' occasional shriek
the girl who missed her connection
the limping loafer
the taxi ramp men
the cardboard holder
professing the no man's land
of a gap between two days
my moon has fallen into

CAFÉ BAR AFTER THE DENTIST

The water-drops are not plastic,
the fountain refreshes
conversation, the rock music
is tinged with the waterfall
that soothes the crashing crockery
and the till-changing hurry.
This impeccable corolla
of splash-controlled drops
is like the smile of my newly fixed teeth.
It does not permit sadness

Here we are, somnambulant visitors
snoring our visions of acceptable travesty
lulled to the sleep of half-life.
Fluorescent cataracts are the perfect romance
like the smile of my newly fixed teeth
that does not permit sadness.

The water-drops are not plastic
at this café called the Goldfish Bowl
but look closer and you will see a rebel heart
beached on a street of carborundum sand
and gasping for the ocean's reality.

RUSTIC WRITER

Writing like a ploughshare through
strands of tobacco with my wooden pen,
the night lies clear ahead,
blank as the head of a bald man,
and I have just decided to celebrate the Now!

Three sand candles eye me
with their flaming mouths.
And what gem is written here
pigeon-holed in this blackest hour?
The world watches with night agape,
playing an invisible organ humming a hymn,
and flickering objects join a jazzed-up version
with my wriggling writhing writing fingers.

Once-fervid foibles rising slow,
bubbles round and grand,
sounds of pianos, circles of the sea.
Old hopes too, gruffly timely,
burping softly transparent green,

For nothing is too serious today,
and all is comfortable shapely rarely-seen
and beautiful in coming forth.

the nature-world is your face-bowl
for washing the eyes open
thereby to sense
the nature-world is a finger-dish
dipped into with the tips of the touch
thereby to sense
the nature-world is this bowl of rice
taste of earth's body
and eat up your fill
thereby to sense
the nature-world is an ocean
which is held in your cup
thereby to show how to drink magic potion!

I bow to the life of all
I bow to the guru in the life
I bow to this dry old wall
I bow to my groans and my joys
I bow to the end of seeking
My cave is everywhere
My cow house is the open road

white raft on an open ocean
white waiting station
where Time hangs its toes
in the heart of the white day
and serpents slide under
plus fund of hope
where sparks fly from

The knowledge tree
of 3 dice throws in a row
is 666 and bingo!
has twinkling leaves of betrayal
excusing you for
being fatally attracted.

Glancing lights of diamond
flicker on their blades
as they turn in the sunlight...
And you among them, dangling,
a little devil of a fellow,
caught on the hop from heaven.

Oh she is so keen
she paws the ground
with restless hooves
she flies to win
and quarrels quick
- argument's O.K.

Oh she is fine
but has no time for love today.
Look I am the last of the lovers' queue.
My waiting work is to be a guard
a companion in a time that's hard
for her heart is like a ragged sail
and she must wind up every strand...

Oh she is so sharp with life
and I am so blunt with ego's death,
she is a knife that sparks on a hammer
and I am the spellbound iron
waiting long and striking not...
can I bear the solitude of her company?

Oh she is a tiger-bird
of flaming fire and air,
all about her is spontaneous fury
including the way she chooses beauty,
and dances confusion in loop de loops.
Oh she is never mine
but she is here and now
and that is a song that is sweet with truth.

There is a corner I know
where the lights of the city
are sprinkled like stars
and domes are easily pervaded by
the rosewater of twilight.
It's a Spanish girl's treasure,
guarded by an unconquered dragon.

There is a window-view
where a girl I know is tempted
to throw out her tresses
to catch a prize prince
as if he were a fish,
and then to let him die
on frozen love's shore.
By the spell of her mouth
tears hang in the eyes
in the form of crystal balls
woven into the careful web
of a virgin sorceress
who lives in a shell.
It's a picture you've painted.

There is a window on the 8th floor.
Up there, a girl I know is a quiet poetess,
who lives in a heart.
In her museum-shaped room
the theory of her is believed
but the practise seems like death,
for words speak out with faint cries
to protest how thoughts plunge so deep,

deep into your shallow heaving chest,
deep as the horizon of your eyes.
And they make her touch tentative,
and her tenderness brittle.
It's a story you tell.

ICE LADY

That puzzling fair lady
(puzzle of my own making)
is a witch mother of prophecy.
She dances a trance of chastity,
so pure everybody has to see.
She artfully beguiles the unsuspecting,
and hangs their hopes in a church.
She seduces them with ice-cold passion
and hides my heart in a glacier.

He was the old man of the sea
and she the flame of female spirit
that flickered briefly in the phosphorus
of her brittle china blue eyes
and the fairy beauty of sheer disguise.

He cried when he saw her disappear
but she was reborn instantly
in his single shining tear
he laughed to see that gift she gave
-   her illusion set him free.

A black beast with wolfish jaws,
and strangely-tapered hairy paws,
howling at strangers in open doors,
this is a friend of mine in hairy form
who has the name Igor.

His fuzzy face that seems made of shadows,
and shiny nose with a scent for toast,
ears which stick up for eyes which hope,
who is this friend of mine I really do not know,
that has the name Igor?

mount the fine steed
with razor blade back
be one though sheared in half
mount her through falling in
the trough of Oneness
mount her without a thought
and be carried to war
celebrate as a daring lover
who rides the night
alone and with no one

Outside my door
scratch the wind´s paws
of uninvited names.
Hopes hatch wings
would fly to the sun
oh if it were not for
that they are of wax
on a day of meltdown
when all hopes die for sweetness

as the wind rattles still more
on this anchorite's door...
Love is so tireless

My heart has deceived me
into believing it a butterfly
free to wander by the way
for the love of a beautiful flower,
but now I know it is a moth
who lives only to die
for the fragrance of the flame
in the very fire of this hour.

Spiritual Life, length of many lifetimes...
You are the time it takes
for the distant star's ray,
and I am the cold lonely planet.

Old God made a new kind
of shaggy dog, called "Me"
One day of thought
and "I'm" the result:
a flaw in the cup of joy.

BREAK UPS

You cry and rain
from brimming eyes
tears of silent pain
to join Love's rivers.

Alone now, I have no rain to fall.
Can only choke in full surprise.
A heart bursts open behind the door
a sudden sack of grief, and more.

One who was injured has no wound,
one greedy grasping has no hour,
one dinner of lust has no sting,
poison has no power now to kill my song
because wisdom flew into my mouth.
It haled from the beauty-jungle,
and fear fell fast away, from wings full of fruit.
The whistle of the warrior for bird
played my heart like a bamboo flute
and cleared my throat of harm.

Beyond the languorous seas of curtain,
within the four walls of a safe cocoon
enshrined in a bottle on a mantelpiece
is the statue of a virgin and a unicorn.

When the door is swiftly opened,
the sudden draught agitates the sea
of curtain that billows and waves...
And the outside world is felt to be present
in a rush of apprehension
as the view back into space is seen.

Down falls the bottle
dethroned by the rampant breeze
and shatters on the mirror floor.
No more virgin status now.
The unicorn of space
has deflowered the safety-net of solitude.

I caught a poem in a time of peace;
a dry old leaf, and I the tree.
What blew it down -this tree's last word-
before making-naked winter settled down?
It was a little gust of Need.

This was the last seat for the hero,
chair or bench, public or not.
This was the last woman for the man,
leaving by a door's sound,
or a place bared in a park's path.

This was his memory of her,
strapped on his chest like a jacket
and crouched in the round of the air
to watch, for all his life.

GUIDELINES

If you wish for a bite of cherry,
be as the little bright boy.
If you wish to never stray,
be as the humble.
If you wish for union in love,
be careful to conquer duality.
If you wish for the fabric of Mind,
have the hat of the correct View.
If you wish for a paradise,
be a meditation practitioner.
If you wish to wear a fancy mask,
choose the expression of your Master,

choose the face which looks at the sky.
If you want a comfortable ride,
turn the snake of change into rope.
If you want somewhere to hide,
go fishing in the midnight inside.
and cling to the moonlit silence.
If you want to be cared for,
go swimming in the ocean of thought,
go hunting in the river of Time
and unhitch the veil from your eyes.
If you want a sense of direction,
use the blows of the world to make you sure,
and leap into space by turning a key.
If you want to be safe,
sit long in the wall of your shape.
If you want to be free of pain,
open its floodgate and consciously drown.
If you want to be a master of rhyme,
be of two minds, but one at a time.

This frozen old morning of icy rims
when the winter mountain silvers,
young almond blossoms in revolt
are lightly trying out a hillside Spring.

It´s like my chin.
The sugar of Age is variously sprinkled.

I am the daylight hoarded in the orb
and plucked like pebble-stones on the drum,
stretched like wine-skins on the wine,
squeezed and drunken, willing fruit
daring carelessly to be tasted.

I'm so full with seeing that my sight is blind
entrapped in vision with eyelids taut,
prest' madly close, clasped with my own eyes,
wondrous full of nothing like bubbles of a brain
on the river of fastest thoughts suspended
into the spell of word-drops on the tongue.

ROOM MATES

A rabbit and a buzzard
lived together in a room.
The bird had no time
for his furry fellow
but only eyes of scorn.

While Buzz dug his talons daily
into his bleeding breakfast,
nervously Bunny Boy sucked his blanket.

But night by night,
his soft soul dreamt
more and more
of a giant beak snipping
the threads that held
him to the mother shore.

42

out of the blue every simple day
swims the sky into this simple place
the distance brims along the wall
smeared there as if it was my painted nose

out of the blue
falls into my eyes
the clarity that knows no disguise
beholds the wriggling out of formless shape
a world called man on the hop from paradise
writhing and pained for being caught naked,
gasping forward, twisted and torturous,
lusting for the beloved hole of its own shadow
to beget more, in spite of all its woe,
of its own kind, the suicide
of the light

out of the blue I am again
I do not follow man
or his train of thought
his mind is met, splat!
for falling through
the bottom of his bucket

his luck is up
when I sweep his room
with a floor-less broom
when my gaze is silver
like the moon

I wanted to wax lyrical for my sister
but winter was very serious,
Life was lean of daylight,
stock was sopping wet in long nights.

A crumb of light could have been a poem
but down the cracks it fell
before I could catch a sign,
lost in the sadness of dank darks.

I wanted to be a poet
for a sophisticated sister,
but tuneless and sullen
and bluntened by the sight of silly sheep,
how was I to angle for a line?

It's a classic O.K.asion
that's woken me out of strangled
doziness into hazy blaze,
out of mildewed weed
laid along this slumbered camp
till the borderlands of another street.

It's a good game Catwat
my playful furry friend,
that we've been watching
and now can rest for porridge interims

(while mist still rules my brains).

It's good teletime hoorah!
to put aside unsolved hopes
and dribble behind defences
and win with one man down
amid a battery of offences.

ODE TO MY YOUTH

I was born a wriggler,
later given to freckles
and coarse curly hair
in a land of foreign mud.

I was born a bed-wetter
and a silent crier,
a mother's sigh.
My father was a spy.

I was born to be apart,
a lover from afar
hovering too close to the fire.
Wings were sometimes singed.

I was born in the East
and reborn in spaghetti
on an Italian ship of divorce
and sent to grey England.

To live and be strong,
to be sick and not spit,
to pee my pants without saying,
to run from the sound of my heartbeat.

To be an intelligent shrimp,
to be a soul in alarum,
to be uniformed into slavery
as a boarding-school brat.

To paint clowns and be free,
to centre from the wing,
to miss the softness of someone
and swallow endless saliva.

Aye! The purgatory of the yellow card,
the blue of bum bruises,
the wars of chilblains and the warts.
I was a victim of convention.

To write porn books in secret
and be baited by an unintended public,
to have earth-shaking orgasms
and emerge from piss-wet sheets.

To be enraptured by the smell
of oil paint and a vision,
to be trained to think big
by minds which were tuned fine.

To be a flash-in-a-pan of fame,
a face on a telly for an instant,

a narcissus in a travel photo
and sensual and cigarette-proud.

To be an art-student
(virgin of much hoping),
to be something of a faker
with his heart hidden in a hat.

To be an arty-fartist
emancipated in a city of rubble,
to be a squat-liver,
a piano-playing writer.

To be a lover leaving,
to be a dreamer weaving,
to be a romantic feeling,
to be a lonely roamer.

This the season
that made me miss the spring
on a Sunday in a park
strewn with litter.
This strange season
takes me by the hand
and shows me old meanings;
the corner of silence,
the sadness of a woman
who can't be a mother.

One kind of shade under a tree
is like a watchman I carry with me,
unseen like the modesty of an eye
and the love that lets in the light of the sky,
as long as this late day's shadow runs,
and as strict as the number of my time when it comes.

It's the knowledge that makes a wanderer wander,
and a special secret something one can squander.
It's the cook of a blissful meal
(what wise unknowing!)
and a canny hunter in hunger going.
It's a monk on his path of great illumination
a-struggle with his need for sex elimination.

I know of just one emperor
and no other owns me
he rules my heartbeats
in a garden
secretly
he guides my hand
to know the flowers there
he wends my way in the forest
and he always finds me

BOUNDLESS WORM

Failing Salvation,
be advised of caution and contentment...
not-aspiring not-acquiring
the simple earth-worm
is your most reliable transport.
Just as anything is possible,
when for blindness you cannot see,
so the practise of this worm
is boundless

Humility.

In the world down under
which I once dug for with my spade,
there streets are broader, travel longer,
koalas are true, more so than boomerangs.
I was nobbled by the pommel of a saddle,
on the other hand I found a kangaroo.

In the world down under
the skin is more naked in the sun,
the wombat missed in zoo visits
(unlovely lone and grey)
is the traveler on borrowed time,
busting his bits, and not so young.

this is the snail writer with wings
of an old bashed computer
uses word magic to be rich
to give the day its shine
uses old van for a giddy morning
down to town then back to shell
with its million inner voices.

lost homeland
found owner
of ownerless world

lost man
Monfi of old
of lost causes
and wounded love
found a pearl
in the palm of his hand

it was his lost pride
and his found light
of no defeat

A soldier stands watch
ready to shoot
- suspected approach
of indulgent citizen!
My soldier Saturn,
principle of discipline,
oversees my creation urge
and outstretched hand
in loving.
He will sever the smile
from my face, with a frown,
if it stays too long
without wanting to work.
He will take me away
from my heart's cup
brimful with wine of good taste,
if I'm going to be drunk.
My strict soldier stands watch
when I'm lost to Delight;
he brings me down
from the sky of desire
with a quick bullet of thought.
Though once again wounded,
I'm ready to begin
to love by the rules,
and march with the Muse,
without losing the rhyme.

One blade of grass
in all beings' prairie.
Just one sky's dewdrop
satisfies me.

my magic marker
is a squeaky wand
is a crackle stick of wit
is a word winger

enjoys poetic license
makes a teacher into a poem
casts spells on students
(oh keen chorus of ears!)
dethrones idols
joins sparring topics
rewrites the rules

my magical marker
is an ad libber
is also a fibber

I am the friend of my enemy.
I am mad monkey "fun for everybody".
I am sad clown who toys with fear.
I am wise fool for the ready gun.
Terror-less I run the race
chased all the way by Ha!
by my own panic of laughter.
I am scarecrow cavorting on its pole.
I am guinea-pig exultant in experiment
forgetting never regretting
a flag on fire am I
a baby kicking
in a membrane moon.

PACT

I have a derelict body
and you a derelict face

Joining together
a pact could be made
to prevent destiny's laughter

beneath the beam of a smile
unstirred by wrinkles
a new twine of skin emerges

my love is sweet and rounded tiny
like a ping pong ball it bounces finely
but by a lady bat is hit back redoundly

ah that lust so sweet returns defeat
and I to bed with no name to tweet

Little girl of old eyes
exact mouth of no surprise
special way of shouting word-less
special heart of loving
in silence, and of grieving,
do you believe in my believing?

The sky is stronger than your sadness,
the sun so brimming burning
is thumping with a violet heartbeat,
the moon is stealing softly upon a dusky garden.

Orbit me and I will give you
planet children.
Tell me to ask your name
and I will draw you to my game,
I will hitch you to my dictionary
and bear you many poems,
children of the milky sea,
reaching hands upon their waves.

Orbit me and I will paint you as the sun
worshipped on by budding twig,
by springy surge to overcome,
by trousered blade of swinging rye,
music to relax to
by sex and times like these.

When I am pinioned to a velvet chair
by my swimming vision,
will you orbit me
with singeing red and blushing pink
with pure and rampant day
molten in all its hue?
and I will give you planet children
and poems of the milky sea.

GOODBYE MS WHIRLPOOL

You are in the mermaid's bath
reclining artfully in a bubbly whirlpool
surprising me with your musing mouth.
You are the Muse of my day,
old woman child soul-sad
as the bottomless hole that is left bereft.
You are the nymph for suckers like me
her body is for Desire alone,
her heart turned to stone by loneliness,
oh the crone as well that curses men
but gives them to suck as they fall
with the frigid tits of regrets and a lost
motherhood.
And you are the girl-fish,
feet too soft on lazy half-fledged legs.
The cruel blade of land, they cannot tread.

Here again on
Love's brimming hour.
In my heart's jar
A sweet secret of sour.

Came the destined midnight hour
the time for us to be all in one
to join our tails in the moonlight
and pool our joint desire
to swim to be elastic as the ocean
to sip slow on speeding thoughts

BIRD-BEARD

A bird has flown from foes in the forest
and in the secret place of his mind has rested
(a small portion of the infinite sky)
borne on the briar like a dusky moon,
gurgling softly, staring sideways,
two bright pink eyes of surprising sunrise
in the darkness of thought surmise him,
and clothe him with a white waterfall
of wings of nectar...
this is a beard where one dove has nested.

On a piece of paper
a poem remotely waits...
beyond horizons the wind
with clouds is charged
and soon will write them
on the empty sky...

and now I find
some words
are scattered.

don't imagine it's easy
to break the mould of your mystery,
the ever-pouring out history,
don't imagine it's easy

you by the grace of all beings,
you by the wonder of sun,
you by the desert of dust,

you by the elephant's shame
if that could exist,
you by the heaven above
down to the tiniest ant,
you are miracle without blame.

The tide turns, not like the bicyclist leans
and slowly knows his bend of road,
nor like the clouds which swift dismember
and re-collect again to form the weather,
nor like the horns of this mad bull of mind
maddened to a fury by the walls of world...
the tide turns does it really is it true?
Yes something decides and the tide returns,
but while I watch it waits and waits
and like a lake of timeless time it stalls
and all the broken pieces of outside life it heals,
all the coming and going swirling years and days,
the hurry of the rushing hither thither waves,
it gathers in it's old and unseen hand.
This mother of the mother is She,
this special peaceful time of disappearing time,
and I am the old man who marries Her peace forever.

night hours' sweet savour
morning before morning
end before day beginning
peace of the day's end

its glow-worm of light
curls in my soul's rest

I'm a sleepy dodo
adrift on a shore-less ocean.
A kind sir has written me in
today's book of living species.

A board am I
To be stepped on
How hard are her shoes!
How much should I stay?
Why do I provoke
The intolerance of pointed heels?
Come with me I pray
To the meadow sweet
Where the feet of maidens
Do only float upon the soft hearts
Of bemused gentlemen.

I am the daylight hoarded in the orb
and plucked like pebble-stones on the drum,
stretched like wine-skins on the wine,
squeezed and drunken, willing fruit
daring carelessly to be tasted.

I'm so full with seeing that my sight is blind
entrapped in vision with eyelids taut,
prest' madly close, clasped with my own eyes,
wondrous full of nothing like bubbles of a brain
on the river of fastest thoughts suspended
into the spell of word-drops on the tongue.

Inventive poem
release me from inanity
of mere words.
Take for example "Love"!

Elusive Muse
reveal your secret arts,
initiate me please
into this mystery,
"A monk who was."

bodies big and rising slow
beautiful round and grand
sounds of pianos circles of the sea
inviting hearts to travel in
their buoyant domes
rising wholly finely rarely
becoming fleecy soft as clouds
and leaving behind what was divided

You whom I've loved for so long
and cruelly hidden from my own love
and killed and lost and found again
and newly risen from the dead,
please grace this seat upon my head.

lama please stand in my skin
just as it has always been
no doubts exist when you are with me
no head of second thoughts

I am on this lightning path you gave me
of rootlessness of fearless love
of all darkness turned to rainbows
when you stand in my skin

witless and moonstruck
I will wander the lands of inspiration
hearing all, seeing one...
the song of Ah in my heart
bubbling its breath of moonbeams

lama please stand in my skin

a mountain-to-be
who for love of the sky
starts up a slope
the slope of himself,
leaves behind a pile
the pile of his days
and arrives when
he has grown in Your image
and the sun is ablaze.

However I may veer,
within I may vary never.
Though hesitant I may appear,
I do not stray or waver.

However may I seem to change,
like the helpless weather-vane,
inside me wends a path
as steady as a seashore wind,

one threaded in my heart
like a long black hear of Hecate,
obeying the law of deepest need
- the vanishing point in Him.

TWO FOR TEA

Love, You are the sea
and I am the waves
You are the ocean
and I am its liner
You are the ebb and flow
and also their moon
Love, I am the sea too
and we live together
in a tea-cup.

those green bottles of girls
countdown of crashed
tragic comic memories
crumbs glued on eyelashes
sprinkle of blind alleys

Imagination is the child of the navel
born with the eyes of an owl.
He artfully imagines
with equal intensity
the play of good and evil
(fine thread of light
woven in the night of the soul).

Imagination is a child of ease;
he sees circles within circles
of power mysteriously
hatched in his curls.

With a mind for the sky
a heart pulls the cart of
equanimity, surprisingly,
by a mountain that fills the throat,
encouraging and sandalwood-sweet.

Pensive with the blue of the heaven,
speech burns the grum of the ground
and a plume of word-smoke expresses fiery creativity.
Scintillating people are to be found
in the surrounding night.
And I have turned into the wood of mahogany.

With the hand open is the potion poured
With these five fingers is my link to land
(tenuous string of magic) formed,
is my body as a bridge compelled to span
the world, and carry more and more.

Because Imagine!
The life still flowing though the body withers,
the throat still giving though it has surrendered,
the wish to endure thirstlessly that will never wander,
surprising gladness which swells up suddenly one
with Sorrow's chord.

EXHIBITION

I'm a Tarifean sailor of a kind
counting sleepless nights
and clouds that scud above
a prison compound
and live in an exhibition hall
converted from the town lock-up
which is where a bell booms
in a vaulted cell
large as a church
and a mosquito attacks as well
with high-toned whine
so that I can pace more corridors
and count more clouds
that wing on the night's wind
and lie awake between the devil
of a penis I have painted
and the deep blue sea
of the time-old straits
where boats go by
like slower clouds
and magrebis play dice
with their own lives.

Oh funny guinea-fowl how would
we stay upright if you were me?
How, if shoulder-less, will I begin to steer
to find a piece to peck without becoming giddy?
How maintain the sudden seizure of this sprint,
pelting rain-down feet, folding grey wing-pleat,
slapping drolly back dead old earth?
By what strings can we be tweaked
to run so glibly gliding neatly
without once losing the uprightness of our
panic?

Oh funny guinea-fowl, how would
anyone believe us if you were me?
Bird bottom of the fancied league
(of peacocks ducks and doves),
raw scraped neck and pinhead cheek...
And you dare to seem so wingless,
parading like some circus freak
a body looking bleak as nickel
dressed in ash-grey feather of burial.
No wonder no one wonders if we are good to eat
to chew to stew to fly to shoot
and least of all to breed!

Oh funny guinea-fowl, how would
we not be free if you were me,
carried along on feet of panic
yet standing still where others fall,
how would we not be free!

On my terrace I have a squat
to mark the time between now
 & once in Laurel Grove
when Linda a Leeds lass
was a song amiss

up rises memory tree
of rusty bed-spring crown
from the roots of bodies squashed
in their tiny tele room of Laurel Grove
its leaves of once-mattress
like neat curls of space
tinkling all in a row of days

up up up to now
via stem of dreamer's pipe
to my squat upon a terrace
where swallows swish

The mind of my Western Muse
is so old that it refuses to yield
fruit which could be signified "poem".
And in the height of its summer,
it's so cold that it seems like a grave;
in the deep shadow of conceptual categories,
its mythical Hen is scrawny and lean,
its egg-laying lifetime soon exhausted
by fierce competition with the factories.

The comfort of my inspirational Muse
is so hackneyed, so shackled by word,
that my shame is as great as Canute's
(note; the King that was dethroned by the sea).
Now a new voice of laughter
has boldly appeared, like the grot
which is under the bed;
has proclaimed Life as a living disaster,
which needs not a single word;
and the mind of my Western Muse
is like a radio that's gone dead.

steep remote street
a ship's deck drunk
its white cliffs of walls
looming as one reels
in the dark night of then
down the tunnel of history

that man of Cutar was a page of treasure
and he went though nobody knows where
(and I built him a seat)
later return ticket by patera
with borrowed amulet
and eyes hopeful for bread

today in a garden
by the dome of an oven
nice cakes of money
and ripe gourds of Love
are hung on Life's tree

PORT

When the blood-drop spilled,
it crystallised and distilled
the pain of hard borne longing
and my love was not in vain.
You were the harbour
brought to bear
my heart-drop to port.
You were the cradle of the coast
that made the wandering
roller-coaster wave
a place to wash its thought.
You were the poet's hour,
you marked his time
and held his trembling breakers
in a cup of sweet sand;
his salty tear befriended
as if it were a pearl
fished out of a calm sea-glaze.

A bird turd is a wondrous thing.
It waits upon a melting wing
to land in the lake of its origin.
It waits for me, and on its heavy weight
I sit my arse more tight
and fly to Creation's sky.

In between my messages
you silently weave yours.
I speak of freedom,
you of safer shores.

In between my touches
I see your lonely body.
My hand is swift
to cross the void,
and speaks in the way
that your twinkling eyes
laugh at vain hopes.

I seethe with loving water.
You breathe of silence
and rest on safer shores.

Splintering via many facets
On the way down a wall
An eggshell head was broken.
Humpty Dumpty said
Why not back a new horse
And change the source?
So I did.
And the egg relived.

A voice is on the tele.
it says it's me and I agree.
If I'm sweet I turn it up,
if I'm sour I turn it down.
A bird above is on the wing,
it says it's me and I agree.
It soars when I am glad,
it trembles when my heart is caged.

Between us a gulf, a meaningful gulf,
before me a tower of silence,
the sound of your silence,
around me the breeze,
the summer silk breeze
breathing many words and whispers
which the silent tower seals.

The night in this day
has invented this play.
Separation is the theme
and I am its actor.
Truly, You are the gulf,
and I'm never apart...
But for this one song,
when will I hear from You, my love?

On my unsmiling horizon-heart
I pour out the leavings of my day
and count on what might last
though knowing that no desire can long
endure that level gaze of calm.
Hurry for the time is short
and Love is close to ruin!
From one fair-scented whim
I bid adieu and court another tune.

I knew a man
listening to aeroplanes
droning by.
He taught me
to be at peace with walls,
to walk on floors
made of sky.

He taught me the art of freedom
which isn't lost in the jungle of mind,
where snakes are just spooks,
hearts are slippery but fine.

I followed a man
and his flute of the mountains
and my blood flowed a blue song.
I followed this river
of a man into the sunset
and I swam in the bliss of the True.

There's nobody fishing here,
there's no-one who is fished.
The water has fullness
but doesn't have fish.
The man has a purpose
but has no wish.
No bait. No catch.

Silver net thrown,
a-hiss it arcs out.
Now through it seep the waters,
down fall heavy drops of rain
as of summer showers.

The pond is really brimming, dark,
mysterious as if the night itself
was spilling from its face,
and he the witch, the deathly watchman;
but really he is just the gardener
of my private heart-pond.
His job is simply weeding.

from the cold egg
came cool dismay
came the clothes of flesh
came the wavering darkness
came the hardened heart
from the cold-born love
came the acid test
came the misted will
came the smiling cheek held in check
and cunningly I still hid my heat
from the boiling day

I said plunge the thought into the flaming water
its mildewed strings into the lava flow
its rambling notes into the whirlpool of blood
boil the old away I said and pour off the poison
boil the dark today and skim the cream of sunrise

for I grow warm as I know my way
the firebird is fledged and flies the nest

the mirror is looking
at the smirk of destruction
and is asking if
this proud man of doom
is really what I am

the mirror is staring
at the cold wind in my laughter
at the dice which roll in my eyes
it asks who is this who plans
with the dearth of his heart
and snaps the neck of the sweet dove
that was given to his hand

this is how you my mirror wonder
what I have done with my smile
today when love has the glisten
which shines in a tear
when fate is twirled round the edges
of the mouth rich in its wreckage
when fireworks are caused
by a strange coolness of the veins
and ice invades the continent of desire

The ragman came.
The band didn't play.
My old man died today.

LIFE-ARROW

the auspicious arrow
tied with ribbons
has no target

the suspicious arrow
of school conditioning
the stick of conditioned thought
snapped by my mind's hand

the arrow that is fired
and does not fall ever
becomes a feather
because space holds itself

The world ship did not sink so deep today,
for one old man has no more weight
of skin and bone and feet of clay,
but sky and space and window-light,
one man less, one star more,
and Hope to float the world away.

A Muse lives in her pleasure garden
and plucks her full ripe notes secretly
on the singing harp of a mouth.
She banishes the pile of my time
made of rumpled leaves of sleep
and reveals what truly emerges;
an implacable arrangement of cones.

Above is the breath of all arising,
the fresh shoots, the blossom
and the rose, and rabbits
that put away their fears
enjoying the spirit of the sun...

Below is the stone of all depending,
the old roots, the cold heart
and the thorn, and night is proud
in stupendous silence.

listen in among the whispers
you have eyes of passion
lurking under dreams

listen fiercely to the future
angel hordes of passion
invisible wings of love
propping up the skies

listen to the secret stores of passion
come from the cupboards of the darkness
storms that burn the cruel smile
from a face
winds that whistle in the holes
of a perfect mask
rains that brim in a needy cup

Oh fire-horse of Love come down
to this little baby I have found
in the mud of a battlefield
and carry him up on your roundabout!

Oh fiery fairy-horse come down
to this little bald man I am now,
so deeply young, so sadly still,
voice that doesn't ever tinkle
laughter turned to angry growl!

MARY MURK

Where is your gift of sight, oh Muse?
Except you wear a face of grief
I cannot find the fire of inner worth,
except you show my own blindness in your eyes,
I cannot see, I cannot see where I have erred.
Please cast a glance into my heart, Remorse,
and fill my mind with your sudden sight,
lighting up all my folly with scorching gaze...
burn me now, and lead me to the light!
A rigid rage of love I will bear,
to strike me dead with meteorite,
dead to the world in strict repose.
A million million miles of stillness-hours
I will meditate friendless and alone,
if you will give me your blazing face,
and become the lightning of my heart.

All went with the hungry river,
my hunger appeased by its own hunger.
The cries of my need flowed from my mouth
and joined the torrent of all others' need.
Washed away forever was the pain
of all the world along with the sound of mine.
For this river of Time was transcendent OM.

One kind of going
is the whistling of the warrior,
every fantasy unmasked
adds another trill to his tune;
his song has a blade
which cuts the sleep from awareness.

I prostrate to the marvel
of the discipline of the yogi;
no outer stage is his,
nor hankering for drama,
he just sits and he stays,
replete with stone stillness,
expert of mountain technique.

I rejoice in the song
of the heart which is empty,
cautiously I sharpen
the blade of its tune
and unfasten my wings slowly
to alight on the peak.

COMBAT

Withering dark forces,
growing sweet light forces,
age-old slow-motion gladiators
are fighting in my heart's stadium.

One is always young, the other old.
The elder knows the end ahead
but the youth never stops to think of Time
because he's free of boredom.

Silent-movie actor,
laurel-leafed toga emperor,
has age-old indecision in his hands;
one sticks its thumb up, the other down.
Who wins depends on what mood he's in.

stick in the shine
resisting the tide
the pull of the flow
the wishes of below

stick of pure will
dislike of history
disdain of gravity
pure vertical trajectory

note:
sticklers for order
are dry old sticks
and not of this kind

Oh poignant is the trembling line of my control,
turning out and turning in, tangling in threat and love,
striking dumb with the sense of danger,
glistening like a snake on voyage through the night!

Witness a wished-for death by wish-bite,
a whiplash of the lip curved on a jagged rim,
eyeless as a tongue, and withering by its look
newly arrived hopes that are waiting for the light!

Calling mouth control, compact kiss of arduous length,
the scorpion's tail that stings by invitation!
When pierced by that heaven's hook I become the catch,
the heart that is fished for exclusive dishes.

My mind is a one-piece jigsaw puzzle
that desires to be puzzled by a sage;
from nought it becomes flame.

My mind is a juggler of particles
inventing the length of a day
transported by the thrill of the night;
from nought it creates.

My mind is a wheel made of numbers
spinning the names of opportunity;
it whirls for the love of its stillness.

I live in a chrysalis
of butterfly-stone.
Will be reborn to give
as a diamond-cone.

Noon-day dial strikes no shadow,
waits for no man as his friend,
drives the point of heaven home
with no encircling sentiment.

Noon-day hell strokes no more waves,
no more welling realms of bitter-sweet
or vague remains to haunt my eyes
with the eternal dying of the days.

Noon-day blissful rings no note
that earthling music can imitate,
rains down sunrays like a crown
for the one who would be lion-hearted.

the great sea-factory
is all around my ears
it weaves a whispering wall
it clasps and heaves
like a lover's waist
it makes mermaids
swim in my dreams
it echoes in the belly of a whale
it draws this hermit into his cell
it grows the secret pearl
inside this oyster-shell my head

Wisdom irrepressible
as the molehill on the lawn;
brutally inexpressible
guarded secret of the mole;
wonder inaccessible
to the ignorant who seek
sleek ego-lawn
- free from wisdom's hills.

On me, a skinny sapling,
leans a ladder full of sound
(a messenger is always
running up and down me,
in and out of visits
to other places not so lonely).

This tree isn't shaky
but has flaky bark
peeling of its old torn wings
every new day, every turn of the way.
And a mixture of many faces and lost boots
hang down from me,
while I loiter.

But behold!
A tightrope walker
snake-like stalks
his essence of mind
upon my spindly branch
and gives no quarter!

The lord of this chamber
is a star and his lady a zigzag:
united, they are the dance of the lightning.

This lord has entered the womb of her earth
and with a light step up its winding hill
has planted the seed of a gossamer thread,

a fine line of perfect escape
to weave into my labyrinths of sleep.

The heart is heavy with its fruit
and the man clasps them close in his hands,
anxious lest they slip through and bruise.
Death has scored again one old afternoon.

In a looking-glass of light's hardness,
cold in the pocket of my memory,
the remote face of a woman looks at me,
ray-lit by some slow stream of blood-light
poured into the mirror of living form
which asks for Love to free her.

I am the borrower below,
my ears as wide as the floor.
as it whispers and creaks.
She above me walks in my head.
I cannot help but catch her sadness
in the cracks of her joy,
I cannot help but hear her sigh
I cannot help but be her spy.

A drawing described the dance of two moons;
chased by the crescent-shape of the other,
they danced into a violet haze of delight
sucked in by a spiraling swirl of the night
touched by the pink stamens of mutual bliss.
It was but dream, and the drawing awoke
into the morning of actual ego's terror.
No sweet stamens, but cruel fountains of
magma,
breath of the depth, in love-scorching streams,
lava of incredible hues, feats of vermillion,
creative power, shot with life and its death...
This was the vision-emptier of my page.
It was no longer you that I met, it was the dance.
It rubbed us out into the night of blue stains...
finally here we are cast as moon's willing
victims.

the Spot
it is always in the wings
waiting for the cue de force
the cri de coeur of him.

sometime
it's ready when he's most awake
(Us...we were always in his wings
but not called upon his stage)
it will leap into his mind
like the scorching of a noon-day.

enter!
the foolish Indian brave
walking down High Street Monotonous
looking for his lost love
- it was his dog he thinks,

but it's Us...we were always in his wings
and in armpits and in skin!
we are his dreaded spot
his dreadful truth,
his revolution's drop,
his flower of compassion-doom,
latent in all his bloom.

The world and my face
meet at the tip of my nose
go into a vertical spin
become one single jelly
and then snore like a train
when I sleep, I suppose.

my sacred view is
a piece of You
a mirror sky
a tunnel through

my sacred view is
my heart that shows its face,
a tiny trembling leaf
in the lull before a storm.

The one I love
will listen with me soon
to share what aloneness
never understood.

I am fathered,
the son of a skeletal tree,
more wary after the withering winter
heart-bare, well-honed.
and joyfully kicking
unneeded leaves.

FREED UP

My mind is like a whore,
she goes with all the men.
I have no way of controlling her,
she desires everything.
Would you put a rope around her neck,
and make perhaps a useful cow?

I'll not
I'll leave her on the streets today...

DAYNIGHT

World that spins
(true time of sunrise please!)
world that hides

within its motion's disguise

thickened by thought
its darkness is drawn
across the face of a day again

to wait for light to quicken
in the moody womb of ourselves
with the dynamite of stillness.

oh glory is the guru embraced
cause of my severed head
our hearts enlaced infinitely
in one space tasted gloriously

I was the cup of the ground
and he the rainy cloud
who filled me up
till I was overflowing rain.
I was the belovéd man.
A heart outpoured its gift.
A voice of heaven roared.
Blissful wings carried my sea of skin.
A rainbow extended from my hand
in five perfect points,
I was made as a bridge
enthralled upon the height.

You gobble me up, kiss the numinous,
Shout with a joyful exclamation of flaming brows,
Catch fire in the depths of my sticky passion,
Whisper Yes! on the path of all creation.

You are the arrow of the plane
with its thunder wings.
You are the claws of the sky
that makes tendrils of my skin.
You are the yawning height
surprising song of thrilling blood.

The boat of vision is Your eye in mine
setting out its oars with a gentle rhythm.
It defines a day throughout the dark,
blue deep below brimming high,
great bowl of sky leaning low,
conjoined in bliss, and only I between,
now with no more mind for gloom,
no place to stand on and say no
because the heaven and the abyss
are one in the vision of this moment.

Where I live it is very plain;
it is taut scope of land's brow
cold damp hand of piled-up hill
simple earth and simple sky
steely winter, one for work;
for living, just the barest shell.

Where I live it is like a stone
that bruises deep, right to the bone.
Unless I am wise I am like a baby howling,
clutching a mother made of skeleton
and afraid of dying.

The time she gives
- an opium poppy.
What's more
her face is my front doorway.
I leave and enter
via fleeting glimpse
between two appointments
on her timetable.

Do you, sofa, hear my bleat
as I lie upon you a crumpled heap?
If you do, remind the tele to glimmer on,
remind the day to be on time,
and everything to be usual as per norm,
I have a builder's job to keep.

I like you am wandering
one against all the dark:
footfalls mouth's balls
words hesitated
suspended
crossed

From crags of dejection,
spring of water's harmony.

From cliffs of mistakes made,
ebullient songs of clouds.

Upwards leaps one pinnacle,
persuades me to Your palace.

So down falls the rain
of washing pain transparent.

In my heart is a huge holiday hotel
- staff on holidays so no room service.

In my lazy heart is an intricate house,
walls and floors all made of glass.

Staff on holidays in other hearts,
but in our dreams they're still here
and we're also on their holidays...

For everyone who loves anywhere
is both the host and the guest
of the dream of anyone else.

In my transparent house I have a bath,
and in my dream-hot bath I have a ship.
And on board this silver ship I have a hero
who hoists my heart's sails inside my house
inside my heart itself where there is no wind!

But still the days glide by without a hitch
spite of there being no room service
and sailing with everyone else.

The ancient and monumental tower of silence
is the towering of the void
though one sees it not.
It spans the space
inside this mind
by the arch of years
poised across the valley of the Esk.
It flies by the crow's mission flight
above the yawning chasm
and dictates a total life.

Impossible to stop
One toes the line
How do you do?
How you stand
is who you are.
Do you dare
be here go on
when words are liars
pictures are just trying you on?

One solid swing of the foot
for ten short thrusts
of Life's knife.
Age-old stint
of games with ladders.
Cold of unlovedness

like the grip of a vice.
Too brief are the climbs
for the falls
water-pores where one can
profoundly drown
until the breathing of Hunger
is more short
more reasonable it's felt.
One toes the line.

To the blind black cat
of plaintive walled-up eyes
and white dot of tail
who wanders in the night
to find me, I owe a debt.
For she is a sign of light
when all is painted black.

This sleep walker of the cockcrow sun
comes on the morning of his ignoring
gliding in the glint of the dew-grass,
spring on the tuft of his moorland,
a sleeper wild and boundless.

While she his bride lies full awake
deep beneath his hill of sleep.

from the beginning
to the very endless,
a road wends its way
among fields of flowers
stretched out to a horizon
with the curves of a smile,
and here is where I wander
and wars of love are fought

My book of braile
is a cat in the dark;
fur for fumbling fingers;
tail to twitch (oh hark!)
for blind man nonsense talk.

2 cats here
one is furry
one is skin & boney
who might that be?
I am the quieter purrer
the stronger snorer
the one who writes the story

A man of no clear address
Is this my place he says? as he daily sits
Am I the crone of this corner? he croons,
as he plies his trade in a tucked away street..
His work is writing down the days.
And of all this remains only the last page
and somehow he has to live it and to give it
and unfist his counting fingers in the shiny waters
and remember his swimming feet...
then at last he knows where he is.
Now a kind tomorrow will roll down pain drops
over the edge of his tiny table
into the river of hungry rain in his pocket.

The girl has a hoola-hoop,
the boy has a loopy hat...
their love is headlong
for romantic seasons.

Window in a cheek
is his lover's bird song.
Blue face with pursed lips
is of course her broody hen.
Dominoes played by a scale
tipped towards disaster;
that's the chance it might go wrong.

My feet are tingling to go,
because my heart is crying in secret
because my love is prancing in vain
in the swish of enamoured grasses
with steps of fairy sweetness,
and cruel day makes my tears shy.

His Muse became the Guru.
He learned to unlearn,
he learned how to glide,
he learned not to churn
with propeller-like mind
and nose-dive into work
and be the slave of more time,
he learned how to float,
how to sip his life subtly,
how to heal the age-old rift
between the sun and moon.
He became skilful and quick,
and peaceful and slow,
and glad not to need.

ODE TO A SCULPTURE

You old fish
chewing dat nut
nitty gritty nut
and the dissolved man
you awfully swallowed
is inside you
and farmed in the tracts
of eternal intestinal space...
And all was planned out.

Friend of an e-mail name,
you're always more
according to that address.

More than a little girl in hiding
and more than just a father
talking in your voice.

More than a woman with a cruel agenda
for soul and shadow fighting.
More important than a thousand ships,
More than your wavy nose is daring.

More than I have ever known you..
Elena punto Eres Mas.

Today I found some tears;
they were old ones stored away
in this pair of borrowed feet
that paddle in memory's pool,
their toes all streaked with slimy brine
and tiny stars of pearls glinting fine
among the gunge of distant woes.

A rose found on a street
reminds me of my own heart
so I put it in a vase
take off the cellophane
and there it still stays
like some symbol of love
no longer abandoned
slowly shedding petals
of my own dried blood.

Oh small am I who protests the sky
and wishes for a cupboard
of sadness instead of space.

Oh tall is the man I would be
who loves the lady and all her fruits
knowing that she will wish them his.

A verse for the lost ones
for the stranded travellers
for the mislaid moments,
those heroes spurned.

A verse for the bombed books
for the defaced looks
for the sweets prized
unfairly out of tiny fists.

A verse for the rejected stories
for clever words despised
by computers' prejudicial memories
and tomorrows forgetfulness.

A verse for the play I played
and the childhood a giant gobbled
and the pages too faint to read
in the falling light of a final day.

Falls the sorry slave of love
into the abyss of his slavery
loses his way and his wits,
and burns until all that is left
is the leafy pond of a heart
from where all new life emerges
and like the mythical phoenix
he is reborn darkly, dressed
in the feathers of his own ashes,
and lo! where his head was
is an offering bowl of his own skull
and where his arms were
are wings of the gladdest giving.

blaring car-horn
as heart's tuner

fish-man's cry
spells Land Ahoy!

swim to mountain
via ocean terrace

this wind a-roaring in the pine tops
with joyful uplift arises from my roots
for crows to laugh their wings
and shouts to match their feats
for sentinel trees to sway though sober
for river's liquid leaden but glinting weight
to hurtle by held within its banks

The world is hanging
rain tendrils on the mountain,
and eyes for green
and fish for flowing hearts.

TRAINRIDE

The light playing softly
on the sad woman's cheek
belies her taste for kinky fashion.
Ex-army is here too
with a mouth like a slash.
Ipad exec mirrored by shelf of perspex
(his name might be Woodpecker)
taps his screen busily.
A boy wriggles beside me
plugged into play station

sucking sweets and texting.
We're all strangers in transit here
and about to diverge
into different chapters.

it was late after a long hot day
in the evening's dim light
when the ground had a glad thirst
for a cloud to be burst from somewhere

it was a film of my own misty emotions
with their smudgy flowers of vapour,
their spray of a million tiny droplets

on lake Taho
fish popping like specks in your eyes
bats blind
all lake pushed into charcoal-grey
mountain
old steamer
man flying

scratchy sounds of my deva ruminations
above unseen a plane reverberates
the distance is like a jar of crystal
a letter Hung is like a fish
the starlight asks
the pine insists
deeper still I sink inside
a river runs in untold telling
its different streams of notes
are joined for one more time

REWALSAR DRAMA

sea fury is locked
within the rippling waves
of the rolling thunder
resonant within
its glass jar of heaven
strangely distant
while still mighty
as if heard from far away
and sung in chorus
with other thunders

the scene is set
for grumbling dwarves
and starving nymphs
then onto stage leap the principal actors

their crack-a-jack claps
vying with each other
as they jump from east to west
and surprise the dumb lands below
with their pitch and vertigo
and intention to frighten

rain applause is rapid to follow
dripping loud big drops
of all colours in grey...
but the party of Rewalsar hills
is a quickly passing play
for here wind takes all
and soon this theatre of sky
has become yesterday's cloud

Hail mount of mountain
steed of stillness
& fast slow time beat
eternal watchman
with mantle furled
silence for brooding over
& lovelight dawns
& stars of ascent!
A dappled beard of snows
crowns your strict repose
sheer above, tall & fine,
knife to slice the sky
and shred the cloud.

Soft spring rain falls.
Wind can play draughts
and ignore winter's commands.
Heart can play bird-songs.

this reedy rounded pond
is like a mother's lap
in it vomits all nature
seethes deeply
and breathlessly erupts
finds my rest
in days of swoon
it macerates its wine
its soupy molder
its red dragonfly
and green frog
legs spread out to dry
its nurtured stillness
of yellow spume
and sound of trickling taps

on this ovoid pond
wishing womb of every day
litchened yellow
deep green wallow
amid shoots of wort
and nights of frog chorus
wisdom may hatch
in wishful eggheads

layers of sound folded
into distant roaming inside of shells
walks for no purpose except
for dots and profiles against the sun
fleshy sand agleam with low tide´s sheen
beach for endless combing
embattled remains of washed up wars
and all zipped up by trim horizon

parrots squawk argue-talk
cane leaves rustle
smooth things over
sunlight rules and divides

Today the door's ajar.
Jungles can be invited in
to hum in chorus
with the central-heating pipes.
Draughts can tumble with the breezes.
Hearts can swing on hinges.

The lush blue bullet train
divides lands of rainy hills
with their dice of scattered sheep.
Two nuns are bound for a holy island.

Allelujia Om!
This is my blue kingdom,
my Indian situation.
An ocean room is wide.
A wooden creaking floor is home.
A moth for no hungry beak
is secret meditation.
A balcony for the rivers roar
and the crows nearby to caw.

Stage-set; the rocket ship of two.
All aboard are heading for space,
from the loins below to face before,
gleeful as the bees to their flowers.

rubble in the stomachs of loins ungirded,
unwound streaked skies of pale blooms,
I the wonder am who knows not his own miracle,
the clouds' graffiti of your hills and sweet clefts.

the stiff legs of the morning
down the road shambled slowly
in their own time
while crows fetched their twigs
and the valley ever brooded its seasons

By fronded walls of rustling cane
by sea-wide views and sandy dune
in tourist mode of bottom rung
a renting's made of makeshift room

the cat was batty
the wind levante
sunny but cold
mind all over
the still place

skidded away into the night
the pair of bogies
that were impatient cars...
we are left behind
alone for the floating sights
in a kind of aeroplane's dream
(hills have ceased to exist)
broken all of sudden
when a village leaps out of nowhere
nested in the lap of darkness
vestal virgin white
strange as an apparition

eye to catch the wave
of the long summer grass;

hand to pluck the leaf
without spilling the dew;

ear for hearing the tune
of the early morning's hour.

ACCOMODATION

I am here for the windy waves
for the sea and its jeweled plain
for the whispering cane
on a path of swords and spears

In my room of C
upstairs beside a tree
here to watch intently
duck mating procedures
and boisterous bills

Vertical house upon a village hill
creations are born of its innocent oven
and blades of coloured rain are forged
to strengthen the cause of Imagination.

barrio chair
mixtures have made you
poet has saved you
gnome has owned you
bottled tree has grown you
bumps have aged you
on my mongrel stair

form and emptiness
intertwined lovers
since Nature began
lips pressed to lips
twigs hugging empty
squares of space

roaring above
the aeroplane
joins the ether
doesn't break silence
completes the embrace

Let go to the road
between two strands of music striving
to the cows the beggars
the rickshaw peddlers and the sellers
to the tourists young and loners old.
To the street where all is sold
let go, heart playing violin with the eyes,
watching the world go by
in all its guises, loud and lame,
sad and sweet.
To the plain maid's face
add a touch of red lust's paint,
To the crusty dreadlocks of Israeli youths,
entwine the hidden oily braids of Sikhs.
To the stumps of arms and legs
without hands or feet,
add the fingers painted with floral signs..
For the cows give banana skins and human
praise.
Offer palm leaves to those with fallen arches
who still stumble ever on.
Let go this outmoded notion of an aim to Life.
Extract a violet hue from the very throng,
and mix all peace of mind with noisy traffic.

welcome to a piece of India
to this babu both old and young
watching as he drinks a chai
blistered nose of someone's cow
cardboard-eating bull moving slowly
dexterous throws of daily papers

rolled up & plopping into windows
with smoke puffs in the morning sun

wolf whistles for bus motion in reverse
Hindu children practicing parade
bells bird-calls cries of all kinds of commotion
dustbin lorry clanking and roaring
& feeding fish squirm at a lakeside
strong puja horns groan in the dark
bright robes or sadhus' painted foreheads shine

a hundred thousand things glitter
as they whirl in the spectrum of mind
Krishna mirrors himself ad infinitum
here comes the Shiva trolley and its gong
plus tiny worshipper on emptied street...
milk left untouched may be a worshipful act
the benefactress is a simple peasant goddess
her smiling face soaped up into a morning
lather
the four sacred footprints of the elephant
are foundation holes for telecom statue
squarely dug and minutely leveled
with dynamited rocks and cries of warning
karma ripens by an act of magic
even as Progress brandishes ugly teeth
meanwhile the oxen plough the little field
hard on the heels of the recent harvest...
lovely is the headlong race of the seasons
the girl in the sari with her bag of seeds
lovely also is the wakeful wind
that ripples the flags & makes
the prayer-poles lean.

VETERAN

Age thirty and all my teeth were rotten,
I had them pulled and they're all forgotten.
My wives are dead and gone too
and my home is an empty bar.
Day to day is not so bad.
Breaking up old bread for the chickens...
Eyes skinned for all comers especially
of the feathered kind...
Don't get me wrong, I Want always gets.
See how my gnarled old but randy pecker
knows when SHE is right around the corner.

Little Mima
can tell the future from peoples' palms.
Having lost sight of her husband,
she jumps in and out of different men,
hauling behind her a troupe
of grown-up children.
Inside she longs to be alone
on her favourite mountain
to watch the dewdrops
of the morning as they glisten.

TITANIO

once a girl with a tenderness too absolute
needed a strong strap in her cheek
made of titanium, white and as light as wings
result: her smile flew faster and for more men
and her love never needed to land

SOUL

She lives on the side of a Kentish hill.
From time to time comes the day
that makes up for a lifetime of delay,
a bird to bring the glad news
that all is not lost.
Life pecks anew on the window
of her sleeping spirit.

He chose from the first
the family profession
of pure philosophy.
It seemed the wisest option.
Knowing that every goal
 is only a wandering cloud,
is at the very least
not to fall foul of potholes
on the slippery slopes of Fortune,

for with every slightest slip
a good student of Life
will change his chip,
his goalposts also,
and mend the broken.

Little old Maria makes her circuit
in the empty plaza
and goes to mass every day or so.
She is neatly dressed always
and has a merry wrinkled face.
Says; "It's true that I've been left alone!"
No need for spoken words.
 (I also saw how they took him away,
shaking like a leaf
in a tremendous storm.
His time had come.)
but oh! I'm so relieved
to be on my own,
free as a waving banner,
as a song on the wind.
And there's always my son in Malaga
to tell me if I'm wrong!"

MUM IN TRANSIT

profile of pointed will
graven in sharpened chin

merman of yore
washed up on alien shore
of hotel sheets

she dreams of Brest

IDONEA

Her mouth betrayed her inner battle,
A struggle long for deeper breath...
Yet her skill was such, she drove a crowd,
She forged a globe, and sent a ship.

GARDENER

She of the goddess statue
is a gardener of souls
but in flesh and blood terms
is thinning hair dumpy cheeks
with chat and smile.
Compost elixir is being mixed
by her in fine proportions
to lay in greenhouse beds.

Gerald
from up the hill lives alone,
son of long gone
very old fashioned
Mr and Mrs White.
Comes down the lane
as he always does
on his sterling old Hercules bike.
Always has a greeting
and the time of day,
he's a good sort
though not too bright.
Then crash bang!
He is all smashed up
by a speeding van,
and his luck run out.
Young Gerald
made suddenly old
now lives away with the fairies
and...

ANON

she is no android
nor fairy nor soul mate
she may be
a bamboo flute

STREETSCAPE

broken down themes
broken down neighbours
with their stony broke dreams
sticking C.D's
with voice wobble repeating
ad infinitum
mind-at-sea seascapes also
amid the lurching of sound waves

STRINGS

Ask the dove, he knows the ins and outs,
the eaves and the pinnacles.
Ask the servant too.
He is master of the house.
And ask the puppet.
He knows best of all
the strings that are moving his hands,
though he would untie them if he could.

OVEN

round apple-like form
containing oven womb,
eyes with tender gaze
made to plunder pleasure,
breasts of falling fruit
scent of garden treasure.

Collage artist collects life
as a shore collects the sea's messages
with devotion for litter...
collage mind collects mind's pieces
and makes accidents remember
and freaks become beautiful
because he is the surprising poet
of the unnoticed beauty
of discarded experience.

THE NEWS

Events rush past in a stream.
Popular uprisings intermingle
with newly established sea levels,
time units are fast and fleeting
and jostle for preeminence
like the bouncing of sand particles
as we gaze on from figurative armchairs,
lounging at bus stops café tables and so on.
Meanwhile a holy and subtle snakeskin
shimmers beneath our feet
and our toes twinkle like stars
where they merge in its eternity...
nothing happens at all,
this is the final irony.

MISTER SMALL

Ages ago it washed him up on a rocky shore,
the sun dried him up into backbone and form...
from then on it was breakfast at 8'o'clock precisely
and the sea never did fall again
over the edge of his controlled kitchen table.
For as long as this little man looked
he was locked in his thought
and as far from the sea
as dry salt.

DEAD MAN'S NOSE

waxed glaze of a dead nose
whitish as if pressed
up against a window-pane
but no

pause button for a video machine
to freeze and numb our frantic wings
our galloping hearts our panic strings

oh that nose whose stopped life
is all of us behind our eyes
and beyond the solid creases
of extinction perfected!

with one click of it we may cross a gap

Ah my mother
My sound in the womb
My song in spite of a cage
My rainbow in case of the cloud.

A meal is served in the mind.
Praise it lest it be forgotten.
Resume chewing, quit talking.

The ocean-drop will seek itself
ferried across in a walnut shell
to find the refuge of all the seas,
to be one free drop in all the deep.

Who can tell what the end of your love will be
when the journey is discovered to be round
and the mind is not captain of its sea
and the distant land is your own ignored heart?

One arose from nowhere
just plays at being there
hides and seeks with faces
in a house of mirrors
someone saw me there

rainbow marbles all
we roll around
on a mirror ocean
clinking glasses
to passing ships
exchanging sparks
of briefest glimpses

A pile of leaves
kicked by passers by
swept in by sweepers
blown by father wind.

A pile of old pages
handed to the typewriter
read down the ages
or burned instead.

A pile is a pile
is a pile of dust.
The last shape
that is left of us.

union of desiring & forgetting
breakwater and flow unbreaking

wave which is never the same
wave called by someone's name

I am made for being unmade
washed along an endless line

Mountain journeys
from valley shadows,
strips the heart
of all its reason,
brushes aside
the clothes of loneliness,
dares wings to fly.

Grounded in way that is secret
by wearing appropriate masks.
Joyful in life as a ferryman,
not fearing the abyss of solitude.

Kill the old dragon of habit
and exit from fear of all gravity;
taste even Now as you fly
away from the Past and the Future.

Seeing the world-to-be-seen
one sees what cannot be seen;
knowing the sky is in everything
- protection for eyes unattached.

Old coins, trusted often.
Sun and Moon.

Water returns the sky.

And Lies?
They are only ghosts
of people that did not rhyme.

this body is a burning house
at the end of a road
but on a wave
found under the skin
it becomes a boat
that carries you over

The white-lake paper
and the poised writing pen
both agree that they are wiser
than the meaning to be written.

Don't cry for the Moon!
Her light is already here.
The Life everybody knows.
She's a whore but has a good heart.
Doesn't ask you to pay.
Doesn't let you stay either.

Open the roof of your eyes
flowers are falling from heaven
gaps in the grim of the world swishing by
swimmers to the swim of playful beauty
flowers are the cups of the skies

Open the petals of your heart

in the open sky
no answer

in the open heart
no question

Everything out is in
The flag is only thought
Sounds are an inner river
Suffering is the clown of Love
Whole worlds make do
on the head of a pin
Everything out is in

waiting
looking

being nothing
wanting to be

immortal.
Distress?

lives that fly
like leaves in wind

your world was never flat
has no edge nor turn
nor time nor even map
sail on, but never leave
circumnavigate a globe
and stay forever close

Respect to the narrow eye of Devotion,
to the line of tempered mind,
repeatedly drawn over and over itself
with ancient fervent motion.
Prayer; a magic power.

Passion is

Looking into
another window
and forgetting
that you're only looking.

Compassion is

Remembering
you're only looking
in the middle
of forgetting.

Wisdom dawns, though very still.
Does not depend on any life,
Does not fasten it with any will,
Is ready as a knife.

Wisdom dawns, one day-less day,
Without a Why? In the world at all.
Then there is no worldly word to say.

Not flag nor room
but home and sweet.
Tent in owls' land,
monk in retreat.

one man went to swim
and he swam at the sea so hard
he must have wanted
to lose his mind
but he never can
because what he gives
the sea will always find

When two things happen
Then two are the one sound
Giving glows with a mighty shout
Touching flows out brimful.
Heart's weeping, never in vain.

Don't kill the sweet songbird
or grasp what you observe
wish to go or long to know
try to make something be

just

flow

let

go

just

hang

let

be

untie the knots that careful blindness tied

On the journey of Life,
Faith is a believer.
Across a tiny pond he paddles,
to the end of the ocean.

A precarious man
is one sucked by a spiral.
Mind touched by the light
it trembles as the wind roars
- a sniff of freedom
on a frail web.
Ignorance clamours for blood
as the spirit faints
in the race of the vortex.
Eyes glazed,
the drowning man
clutches for a straw of wisdom.

The nose of a man
was run down by a tram
on a weekday of weakness
paved with good intentions.

into the vortex of the web of Time,
reborn in the form of a furious fly...

in the space of the centre where there is no"I",
nor residue of cobweb, of hunter and hunted...

the heat of the kalpa's end is radiated

One-pointed sailor for freedom
who stitches the sail of his heart;
opening his mind to the world,
escapes from an inner disquiet.

the tic
is a kamakaze pilot,
he waits until
the warmth of his own ruin,
then he jumps into all beings,
and lays the egg of his life down.

Power is just joy
of being able to give.
Beauty is knowledge
that opens the eyes.
Protection is innocence
before the book of the sky.
Pilgrimage is not to anywhere
but a wide-eyed child.

Snow-drift thoughts equal pile up problem.
Snow-flake thoughts equal beautiful freedom.

The moon in my car window
standing still but travels fast.
Single mind ploughs the sky.

The rain comes down
on the lucky plain
in the middle of a hopeless man.

cardboard house
has no foundation

frightened heart
Journeys in a storm

mother rocks
a stillborn baby

Abstracted Why?
almost pruned to a point
by a pragmatist What?
(the one to reason things out)
gazes out of the window
and watches how the light flickers,
how the shadows stretch...
It's her only escape
from life as a blackboard.

You are the lonesome stone
by the road that leads to none
and no-one knows what grows
by staying so long upon the side
except Love's imperious rose.

LOVE RIDDLE

love fire touch not
till flame can quench

love thirst abate not
till flame can drench

the chill white wind
with claw-like hands
tears the tree
no heart is counted out
we are all one
as leaves and fruit

The mountain silhouettes perhaps in moonlight.
The spiral worth a billion shoots up
and disappears into itself
- but the money isn't lost.

ANON

a genius flies a kite
high above all the roofs of town
and nobody knows him
nor even see the string that he holds

as his heart sings

Grow a lost garden
and hide a heart's rose.
This is the conundrum
a man must suppose.

agitated sound of instant "merit"
sounds like pram wheels on pavement
but is the sploshing of competing fishes
in unholy battle for dharma crispies

Mother Isle
precious body,
rare to find
in an aeon's ocean.

Fear conceived me.
In the tight white swaddling-sheet
I was woken up, I was born.
Jesus was nailed into his human form.

This universe is a gambler
with its all & its nothing
plays for hearts to bursting
and heads that roll faster

One is to raze the lost ground
that's given to fantasy lands;
two is to be uglier now,
not cry but accept what is.

A drumbeat is in love
and answers the drum.
The flower is full of its wine.
Bee buzzes drunken.

Heart-food
is made by itself
but never cold-served.

Contentment!
Ignorance is the freedom bestowed on form.
              It need not long.
Seeking is the curse imposed by Will.
              It has to find.
Limitation is the freedom of our life in form.
              We cannot get.
So like a pig which is tethered by a rope,
by what we find in our small round,
              we rest content.

Caution when you label a can!
What you see here
is a switch in the form of a man
that can only be flicked
by a one-eyed electrician.
And what results is the light
of a woman.

While he sits safe in his role,
she waters the flowers of the future,
free of a debt to the present,
for she is the mother of dreams.

Lovers dive these days
down to gather lotus flowers
painted blue and crazy
to sip the nectar of secret hours.

last room
homeless home
ceiling of eye
floor of feet

Once there was a blue
piece of the sky
that got into the cogs
of the daily mind's clock

and had a way
of making itself important,
something of a flea
in the habitual ointment.

She traps the shadows
with her magic cross
and makes slaves
of errant thoughts
and doubters' webs.

The blue heart
surprised itself
by being locked
away in a chest.
But also it knew the real reason.
Ice had to be broken.
The lid had to be lifted.
Love had to be the best
of the best..

Someone has turned on the blue sun.
It's enough to make a swimmer run
to the other side of a sea
or a moon shy of shining into a room.

A Void
made a brief, bluish appearance.
The beak of a deft diving bird
tapped on that wondrous window,
and it was power's moment,
suspended on a thunder stroke of midnight.

to catch it
is to know a dream
to fish it
is to supper well
it's blue and mental
slippery and eel-like
and easily lost
into the sea of silence
where lost messages merge

A small and random fragment of heaven
landed on the doll's head
and spread transparency
even to the tips of its puppet strings.
Astonished and somewhat terrorised,
she danced in a freedom
that she had never known,
and glowed blue with the power
of being found awake.

Blue leaves are always
an exception;
found only on the hills
of pure Imagination.
For this reason
true sky-growers tend to shun
the humdrum life of normal leafage.

The first baby to walk on the moon
Was blue. It had no fear of rocket-flying.
It was born before pink babies
Had even been wanted.

Charming yogi of artful nature!
Ravisher of blue thought
and tamer of twining Mind.
Master of poison-letting
by letting go.

Destiny in the form
of a great bird
placed him in line.
He was the jigsaw's
last blue piece.
So he hung there,
feeling rather foolish,
waiting to be perfectly fitted.

Man and Woman;
in between, sword of Wisdom.
Cutting loose,
one into two Truths.
"I am around you", she says.
"I am within you", he says.
"I am moving you", he says.
"I make you still", she says.
Lying beside each other
on the bed of Experience;
Truth of two-in-one.

Enigma;
if there was no sword
there'd be no union.

Emaho!
From the centre of Nowhere
Grows a mountain of peace in this pure land
A world not of the world beset with woes;
Peaks of red rock capped with ice,
Mighty heights with endless views,
Bathed in amber-coloured skies,
Served upon by suns and moons
With strands of silver and of gold,
And thronged upon by forests deep
Adorned with necklaces of secret streams.
This is the homeland of all those who know
The Nowhere in the open heart.

I winced in the blood-red sunset
and ran to the Master, crying.
On came the beams of Love,
arrows of crooked thorns,
and crackled in my heart like flames.
I throbbed and ached and swore against
the curse of Love, yet threw myself
again into the pit of feelings' fire,
for without them I was nothing.
"Have mercy on me Love
for You are great, but "I" am vain!"

MYSTERY

To be in the present is to be free from the past.
To be free from the past is to be without a cause.
To be without a cause is to be free from feared
effects.
To have no effects is to have no future at all.
To be without a future is to be without an answer.
 What will I be next year? Mystery.
It's to shout in an empty valley and hear no call.
It's to have no pretence that anything belongs to me;

No past, no future, no plans, no voice, only
echoes.
To be no-one is to share my seat with the infinite.
Who comes to meet me? She is only my non-self.
She is just my sweet heart's face, my love for the lama,
She is just my friend of no fixed address,
The cloud-dancer and beggaress,
The refugee exiled to eternity.

AMALGAM

Once there was an It
that became part of Her
for Him to see the light
that She was, because of It,
and vice versa.

That ancient dance
was a spiral snake
that was also Him
and Her, entwined in one.
Giddily they danced
the modern way,
by swopping places,
and span and span
until no outside was left.

IF-A-SICK

This is the thickness sense of sick body,
imperishable hut built in the fastness,
gloomy resting-place for restless traveller.
Within this prison wall there is a chink
like a butterfly of light upon it;
that flame will burn the paper box of body.
Itself nothing, but still dwell upon it,
key of door made of unconditioned,
magic naked suit an emperor wore.
Mind itself nothing, but dwell upon it,
dancing gold light of the same old wall.
It tricks you into seeing with the blind side of the eye.

THIS IS NOT A BED, THIS IS AN ARGUMENT

To the north against the headboard
of the old campaign bed
of her father's first world war
my mother is occupied chiefly
by the problem of where to lay her head
in another long night time
to play at being embattled in the trenches
with intermittent cries in a sing song voice
like little paper bullets in the void
that mark the time of a scanty sleep.
There she blows, upon the wintry bed,
captive on its deck, and swung about,
in her lone slip of a form
though wide also as an ocean going hulk,
lying or sitting slumped
with swollen legs posted like guards
at the ready for forward action,
or hoisted like gun barrels
slowly upon peacetime cushions
as if to call a truce, and be done with all the slog.

TREE

She Became
A tree of glass and light,
A roundish sweep of dancing arms,
A love described
That lives within,

Is found at last.

SON

Saved by my mum
So many times said he of me
You were the apple of her eye
Said another
Yes I thought
But how I fumed and fought,
Since her will sought so strongly
And it twined in mine
And I was bound by an undertow of time
And we were wounded both
In a gilded cage.
Twin souls are not to be recommended
Is what I replied.

to the station
with the beggar family
on the bus

I am chaff in the whirlwind
of faces and traffic

on my forehead
is the scar that travels
like a flickering lamplight
in a stormy night

The school girl so boyish in her uniform
stuffs it into a bag when she gets home.
Her father is the humble chai maker.
She rains soft loving blows on his back.

Crescents kiss
Spirals bind

Man persists
Owl refines

Comet races
Spider places

Cast upon an unknown shore,
bedecked with streamers of the sea...
deep the blue that married you,
deep the heart that married me.
Praise upon my lips
will never turn sour
for the song is eternal
and the sound is ever-sweet.
You are the poet's love,
you are his strumming strings,
you are his land of long Desire
where he has come to lay his limbs
upon the sand of an unknown shore,
bedecked with streamers of the sea...
deep the blue that married you,
deep the heart that married me.

POEMS IN A PANDEMIC

1

Cupidemia will come.
Nervous eager faces
will strip off their masks.
The flame will surge,
the rules fall down
and blood will buzz.
Make hay, make love,
make babes too while the sun doth shine.

2

People pass me by
masked up to the eyeballs.
I try my half best to comply
and mirror back an apologetic version.
Social distancing is our game
and the referee is our shared obsession.
Did you see? Didn't she? And so on...
Did he transgress the social rule
when he skirted round
a pair of stricken adult legs?
I would like to be a child again!
in his defence he said.

NANNY GATES

Nanny Gates stitches like the wind in her cardigan,
within she sails as has never been seen before.
"This woolen is bottomless," she says,
as if it was the meaning of everything.

Like an old stick of dust she sits and knits this,
Now it's a jumper for John, now a mitten for Ann...
But who would know how within she really is
- a hungry owl hunting in the hollow of hills
for the meat of my living skin!

This is Skin, clutch of her needles,
quick house of robes, for the eyes of eagles to see with,
fields swollen with grain, furs breeze has subsided in,
sea-coasts of sand shrunken to the point of a pin in her
hand
- we grow old and die upon the hem of this globe.
This is Skin, the margin that clings to be filled.

Nanny Gates sits in silence in her cardigan,
within she feels as has never been dreamed before.
She lisps the crumbs of the myriads with her mouth;
"This is quite meaningless," she says,
as if it were the mystery of all meaning.
 Like an old stick of dust she sits and knits this,
now it's a muffler for my sister, now a darning for Dad,
but who would know how within she really is
like a whip that flicks the face of the moon?
Death by no means can snap it for his kindling wood
for this whip is our living Will.

This is Will, which works in the wave
like the carefully-webbed net, power never
guessed,
secret of sea-dark sown in our heart
that drives us on Present Future Past,
drawn in the palimpset of her skill.

Oh my Nanny still knits but in a dead woman's chair,
so still you cannot see a single sign of her life...
like a mast of a ship adrift in an ocean of hair,
with a sail of woolen wings smelling of mothballs.
Brown-bodied dusk gathers in stains,
the old skin cracks in the cold new air.

CACTUS MAN

He's searching for the secret of the cactuses,
leaping from his city swamp to desert, in one jump,
aflame with thirst to drink of mystic cactus dew
its one essential drop.
Will God come out now and teach me how to dance?"
"The Chicken Foot in the Soup Bowl Waltz,
& The Hoof which gallops in the heart?"

Ah but that dance was so victorious
he could not dance

that dance was so wide he could not pass
that dance was so fine he could not grasp
(quiver of this leaping mind!)
that dance was so fast he could not rest
- small and lost and faraway he was
in its awe-full wonder,
a lone shout unanswered in the hugeness of the day
and swallowed in the shimmer
of the mirror-like all-embracing stillness.
That dance was so slow it was too quick,
he could not last,
not like the cactus that is steady in the sun,
octillo, spidery and haphazard,
pitaya-spine, aloof cardon.

How then his brain aged old, its fibres hard and
rooty.
Eyes beheld with empty orb their mind-made views,
Once truths of thought were fallen
from their early morning beauty
and scattered in the sand like worn-out cactus shards.

But because he was so disappointed,
God showed him he was dancing;
slow solo Soup Bowl Waltz,
gallant in chicken-foot style,
subtle entreating fingers of horizons
with xerophyte syllables,
and final-thumping Heart-Hoof,
crying for a midday moon,
galloping gladly for the mirage of an ocean...
and he found in that final dance

on that imaginary shore, the compassion-dew!

The tasting of it was his own boiling with Love's
thirst
and bursting in the bounds of cactus flesh,
and like an epileptic dancer, self-driven to no
return,
he became all the guts he had,
melted by the guru in the sun.

NO RHYME RAP

These days I have no song
no marching anthem
not a whisper
I'm more prosaic
no spite to spit
no bubbling wit
no snatch of tune
to catch me out
no whimsy whamsy
no cutting word play
no Oscar Wildey
no groan of cliché
no glut of -isms
in the verbiage

no fanfaric onomatopoeia
to string my bow with
to woo my love with
to sing a song with
in the shower.

These days I am...no singer
no molly coddler no gusty vocals
no hearty warmer no hollow tiger
my orchestra is all around about me
my glass and spoon a-tinkle
my diet of rainy day drops
a patter on my street of footsteps
my legs for walkies
my cat for talkies...
village life is where it's at
a-brim with great themes
with novios and neighbours
and shiny cars that go to work
– less in times of crisis -
and its dogs as ever...bark.
 "What more do I need?"
The radio and the tele tell me
"Your e-mails flow
in a modest sprinkle,
you're entirely cured of adware
and at 56 with a crop of curly hair
that's not at all a bad life you have!"

These days I have no song
nor disc to play
on supposed desert island

though unaccompanied
I'm not bereft I'm not deserted
no wind to sail with
no wine to dine on
no rhyme to lie with
no sleeves to trick with
no goal for opening gambit
no leap to long for
no hope to hum for...

I'm 66 now
and I laugh silently more often
in the shower.

Write on a page a wordless line,
Sign it, name it, call it "mine"
- that's what we're like.

PROCESS

1

He was sent an invitation
and he replied with invocation,
the situation was serious
and he was never in jest.
Sun entered his doorway
with sharp severe rays,
spoiled his old tricks
of skill in romance
with scorn of desire.
Guru entered his life
with subtle intrusion,
and ruined all his chances.
It was sun versus damp,
wisdom versus illusion.
With the face of the truth
the sun gorged on the cloud
and dissolved the clown's mist.
The sharp ray of the dawn
severed the night's life,
and he was born into daily servitude,
hard work and solitude,
polishing the silver
(reflect the sun if he could,
become a man full of virtue.)
First mistake.
Trying too hard, no humour.
Voice that is strident.
Clown becoming outcast,
vision incompatible.

Away from pain and dissent
into bliss and retreat,
but not without sea-weed
in the freedom of this sea.
Hair-shirted overly extreme
self-abnegation,
cruel to the picture
of the cherry-lipped clown.
Swimming mind of deep water,
fish patrolling the murk,
foregoing the dappled light
and glinting blade of sun
for the shadows of half-honesty.
His new name is Trouble,
a self-induced bubble.

2

The man with the hole
of the world in his heart
made whole by his pain
laughs at the sight
and stakes all his gain
on the apparent absurdity
of thinking self-important.
Flung aside his hair-shirt
and desire for self-saving
so-called spiritual achievement
(acting out of fear of failure
more than growth from attachment),
newly donned his naked harlequin costume,
he laughs with sweet words' lips

169

which cannot emulate sadness
but only stimulate the glad side.
However farcical his comedy,
yet there's no taint of derision.
Delight comes to the rescue
of tragic-habit souls,
caught in seas' shifting murk,
ones he has swum.
Sunbeams of laughter tickle
firm fearful hearts.

He laughed as he gambled,
he died laughing repeatedly.
Growing fun and compassion,
free of self-worship,
advice full of caution,
thoughts full of thrills,
exceptional entertainment
such as jokes from a skeleton,
this clown made a special blanket
for others to be warm in
of all his old tricks
without need for new ones,
all woven in.
He relaxed in freedom's beauty
empowered to spin space
for anyone who so ordered.

3

Illness in middle age
rose up in full alarum
like a poltergeist of tragedy

knocking in clown's cupboard.
Broken plates and china.
Broken outer forms
in an unbroken dream.
No jokes from the sick bed;
Life became serious,
Death, after all,
was no laughing matter.
Boo! says the audience.
Shucks! says the clown,
his eyes fiery and sunken.
It came to him in a flash...
Good and Bad was one!
Shucks! he says again.

Suddenly the sky
fell onto the ground,
Illumination came!
Sunlight ran to kiss darkness,
ran golden into the blood of the river.

Printed in Poland
by Amazon Fulfillment
Poland Sp. z o.o., Wrocław

66327431R00103